MW00986051

• BEATRIX POTTER'S •

Country World

POSTCARD COLLECTION

TM

~•~

30 CARDS

F. WARNE & C°

FREDERICK WARNE

Published by the Penguin Group
27 Wrights Lane, London W8 5TZ, England
Viking Penguin Inc., 40 West 23rd Street, New York, New York 10010, USA
Penguin Books Australia Ltd, Ringwood, Victoria, Australia
Penguin Books Canada Ltd, 2801 John Street, Markham, Ontario, Canada L3R 1B4
Penguin Books (NZ) Ltd, 182-190 Wairau Road, Auckland 10, New Zealand

Penguin Books Ltd, Registered Offices: Harmondsworth, Middlesex, England

First published 1990
1 3 5 7 9 10 8 6 4 2

ISBN 0 7232 3646 1

Printed and bound in Singapore by Imago Publishing Limited

INTRODUCTION

Beatrix Potter is best known as the author and illustrator of the famous *Peter Rabbit* books, but her work as an artist was very wide ranging and encompasses a great variety of styles and techniques.

Born in London in 1866, of well-to-do and somewhat straitlaced parents, the young Beatrix spent a great deal of time drawing and painting. To begin with she copied illustrations from books, but as she grew older she developed her own subject matter. Although she had some formal lessons in art, much of her skill came from her acute powers of observation. She was a frequent art gallery visitor and made detailed notes on pictures and exhibitions in her Journal; she also visited and made sketches at the South Kensington Museum which was conveniently near her home.

Her chief interest from an early age was the natural world, and her meticulously observed and executed studies of plants, flowers and animals show the skill in portraying the animal world which she later used to such effect in her little books. Her first commercial success was a series of greetings cards prepared for Hildesheimer & Faulkner in 1890, and she continued to design cards for many years, often for charitable uses. As she grew older her eyesight was no longer good enough for very detailed work, but she continued to paint and sketch right until the end of her life, even though after her marriage in 1913 she largely gave up her book work and turned to farming in her beloved Lake District.

The postcards in this collection show a range of her landscape, animal and flower paintings and demonstrate the delicate charm and skill of Beatrix Potter's best work.

POSTCARD

Rowing boats at Teignmouth, Devon – a
watercolour by Beatrix Potter
© Frederick Warne & Co., 1987

POSTCARD

Study of carnations – a watercolour by
Beatrix Potter
© Frederick Warne & Co., 1955

POSTCARD

'Spring' – the garden at Harescombe
Grange – a watercolour by Beatrix Potter
© Frederick Warne & Co., 1955

POSTCARD

Study of a grey rabbit – a pen-and-ink and
wash drawing by Beatrix Potter
© Frederick Warne & Co., 1987

POSTCARD

The shore at Derwent Bay – a
watercolour by Beatrix Potter
© Frederick Warne & Co., 1987

POSTCARD

Turk's-cap lily in watercolour and sepia ink
by Beatrix Potter
© Frederick Warne & Co., 1985

POSTCARD

Side entrance to Melford Hall, Suffolk –
a watercolour by Beatrix Potter
© Frederick Warne & Co., 1955

POSTCARD

POSTCARD

View from No. 8 Bedford Square – a
watercolour by Beatrix Potter
© Frederick Warne & Co., 1987

POSTCARD

Oak leaves and acorns – a watercolour by
Beatrix Potter
© Frederick Warne & Co., 1955

POSTCARD

Greenhouses at Melford Hall, Suffolk – a
watercolour by Beatrix Potter
© Frederick Warne & Co., 1955

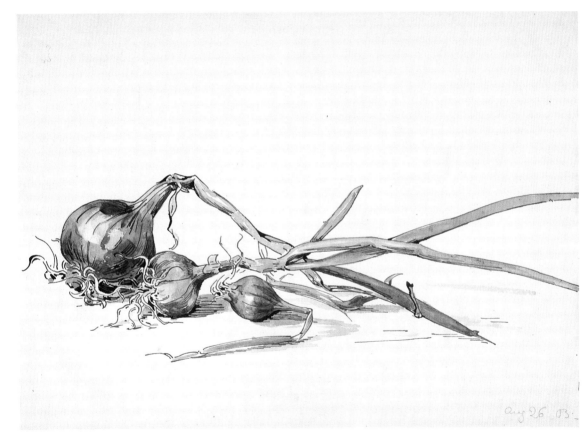

aug 26, 03.

POSTCARD

Study of onions in sepia ink and
watercolour by Beatrix Potter
© Frederick Warne & Co., 1955

POSTCARD

The crossroads at Sawrey – a watercolour
by Beatrix Potter
© Frederick Warne & Co., 1978

POSTCARD

Iris plant seed-pods in watercolour
by Beatrix Potter
© Frederick Warne & Co., 1972

POSTCARD

Waterlilies on Esthwaite Water – a
watercolour by Beatrix Potter
© Frederick Warne & Co., 1955

POSTCARD

Wall at Melford Hall, Suffolk – a
watercolour by Beatrix Potter
© Frederick Warne & Co., 1955

POSTCARD

Harvest at Esthwaite Water – a
watercolour by Beatrix Potter
© Frederick Warne & Co., 1972

POSTCARD

Marguerites and buttercups – a
watercolour by Beatrix Potter
© Frederick Warne & Co., 1989

POSTCARD

Back view of squirrels on a log – a
watercolour by Beatrix Potter
© Frederick Warne & Co., 1955

POSTCARD

Sawrey under snow in watercolour and
pencil by Beatrix Potter
© Frederick Warne & Co., 1978

POSTCARD

A bunch of tulips in watercolour and
pencil by Beatrix Potter
© Frederick Warne & Co., 1988

POSTCARD

'Lakefield', a country house in Sawrey,
Cumbria – a watercolour by Beatrix Potter
© Frederick Warne & Co., 1955

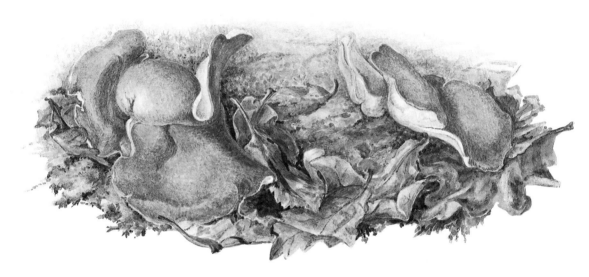

POSTCARD

POSTCARD

Kirkcudbright Bay, Scotland – a
watercolour by Beatrix Potter
© Frederick Warne & Co., 1955

POSTCARD

A group of wild flowers – a watercolour
by Beatrix Potter
© Frederick Warne & Co., 1955

POSTCARD

The kitchen larder at Lakefield Cottage –
a watercolour by Beatrix Potter
© Frederick Warne & Co., 1989

POSTCARD

View across Esthwaite Water in
watercolour by Beatrix Potter
© Frederick Warne & Co., 1978

POSTCARD

Study of a partly opened honeysuckle
flower – a watercolour by Beatrix Potter
© Frederick Warne & Co., 1988

POSTCARD

Rain at Lingholm, Keswick – a
watercolour by Beatrix Potter
© Frederick Warne & Co., 1972